What Did the Cross Achieve?

The Crossway Short Classics Series

The Emotional Life of Our Lord

B. B. WARFIELD

Encouragement for the Depressed

CHARLES SPURGEON

The Expulsive Power of a New Affection

THOMAS CHALMERS

Fighting for Holiness

J. C. RYLE

The Freedom of a Christian: A New Translation

MARTIN LUTHER

Heaven Is a World of Love
JONATHAN EDWARDS

The Life of God in the Soul of Man
HENRY SCOUGAL

The Lord's Work in the Lord's Way and *No Little People*
FRANCIS A. SCHAEFFER

Selected Sermons
LEMUEL HAYNES

What Did the Cross Achieve?
J. I. PACKER

WHAT DID THE CROSS ACHIEVE?

J. I. PACKER

CROSSWAY®

WHEATON, ILLINOIS

Library of Congress Cataloging-in-Publication Data

Names: Packer, J. I. (James Innell), author.
Title: What did the cross achieve? / J. I. Packer.
Description: Wheaton, Illinois : Crossway, 2023. | Series: Crossway short classics | Includes bibliographical references and index.
Identifiers: LCCN 2022046431 (print) | LCCN 2022046432 (ebook) | ISBN 9781433590504 (paperback) | ISBN 9781433590511 (pdf) | ISBN 9781433590528 (epub)
Subjects: LCSH: Jesus Christ—Crucifixion. | Atonement. | Theology of the cross.
Classification: LCC BT450.P335 2023 (print) | LCC BT450 (ebook) | DDC 232.96/3—dc23/eng/20230217
LC record available at https://lccn.loc.gov/2022046431
LC ebook record available at https://lccn.loc.gov/2022046432

RRDS		31	30	29	28	27	26	25	24	23
14	13	12	11	10	9	8	7	6	5	4	3	2	1

Contents

Foreword

I HAD THE PRIVILEGE of knowing James Packer, or "Jim" (as he told me and many others to call him), personally. I got to know him in 1984 when he was at Gordon-Conwell Theological Seminary teaching a class. After class, I saw him alone in the dining room, introduced myself, and asked him if he would like a home-cooked meal. He responded enthusiastically that he would. I called my wife and brought home J. I. Packer for dinner!

Jim Packer would introduce himself in his classes saying "Packer's my name and packing's my game." By this he meant that he would stuff content into his lectures and reading assignments until the students were full with the material. He was a gifted Bible teacher and a master popularizer of Reformed theology.

For many of us Christians who came of age in the 1960s, 1970s, and 1980s, J. I. Packer was our first, and often our best, teacher of theology. He was our guide to historic Christianity. His treatments of the atonement, the authority of the Bible, and other topics were both popularly written and theologically careful. To settle certain issues for myself, I turned again and again to his books, which I would then give out to help others. *Fundamentalism and the Word of God, Evangelism and the Sovereignty of God*, and his introduction to John Owen's *The Death of Death in the Death of Christ* were the first serious theology texts read by many people in my generation. And of course, all of Packer's skill shined forth in his bestseller, *Knowing God*.

All the while, Jim Packer was warm, kind, and pleasant. His mind was always alive, especially with thinking through the meaning of ideas. He often helped students or friends see the implications of what they said, perhaps even unintentional implications. And he did it often with a prodding, Socratic style of questioning.

"What Did the Cross Achieve?" was originally given as the annual Tyndale Biblical Theology Lecture in 1973 at Tyndale House, Cambridge. In this address, Packer dives deep into the Bible's teaching on the death of Christ and its atoning significance. Crucially, Packer is also concerned with how Christians and theologians down the centuries dealt with the question, "Is penal substitution one image of the atonement, or the heart of it?" He concludes—rightly, in my view—that it's the heart.

Packer's lecture was a watershed clarification of a doctrine that he himself had been sometimes criticized for downplaying. In "What Did the Cross Achieve?," Packer engaged directly with criticisms of penal substitution that were effectively minimizing or undermining it. Whereas some scholars saw penal substitution as just one of many images of the atonement used by the New Testament writers (to be considered equally or even as less than the others, such as ransom and victory), Packer demonstrated that all other metaphors used to describe the reality of Christ's atoning death *assume* penal substitution. Packer's great conclusion is that penal substitution is not merely one of a series of images; it is rather at the heart of the atonement itself.

I'm delighted that Crossway has decided to reprint this as a book of its own. It is worth your time to read (or reread). This work, while short, is nonetheless "packed" with truth about the astonishing saving work of Jesus.

Read and marvel!

Mark Dever
Capitol Hill Baptist Church
Washington, DC

Series Preface

JOHN PIPER ONCE WROTE that books do not change people, but paragraphs do. This pithy statement gets close to the idea at the heart of the Crossway Short Classics series: some of the greatest and most powerful Christian messages are also some of the shortest and most accessible. The broad stream of confessional Christianity contains an astonishing wealth of timeless sermons, essays, lectures, and other short pieces of writing. These pieces have challenged, inspired, and borne fruit in the lives of millions of believers across church history and around the globe.

The Crossway Short Classics series seeks to serve two purposes. First, it aims to beautifully preserve these short historic pieces of writing through new high-quality physical editions. Second, it aims to transmit them to a new generation of readers, especially readers who may not be inclined or able to access a larger volume. Short-form content is especially valuable today, as the challenge of focusing in a distracting, constantly moving world becomes more intense. The volumes in the Short Classics series present incisive, gospel-centered grace and truth through a concise, memorable medium. By connecting readers with these accessible works, the Short Classics series hopes to introduce Christians to those great heroes of the faith who wrote them, providing readers with representative works that both nourish the soul and inspire further study.

Readers should note that the spelling and punctuation of these works have been lightly updated where applicable. Scripture references and other citations have also been added where appropriate. Language that reflects a work's origin as a sermon or public address has been retained. Our goal is to preserve as much as possible the authentic text of these classic works.

Our prayer is that the Holy Spirit will use these short works to arrest your attention, preach the gospel to your soul, and motivate you to continue exploring the treasure chest of church history, to the praise and glory of God in Christ.

Biography of J. I. Packer

JAMES INNELL PACKER (1926–2020) was born in England. As a boy, he suffered a severe head injury that prevented him from participating in sports. Taking refuge in books, Packer discovered his intellectual gifts, and while a student at Oxford University, he was converted to Christianity. Shortly afterward, he discovered the writings of the Puritans, whose emphases on the trustworthiness of Scripture, genuinely transformed affections, and earnest pursuit of holiness deeply shaped Packer's life and theology.

While working in Christian education, Packer wrote a series of articles about the basics of the faith for a small evangelical magazine. These articles were expanded and adapted into *Knowing God*, which became one of the bestselling Reformed Christian books of the century and established Packer as an influential theologian and teacher. Packer's teaching and writing ministry grew in influence, and he became one of evangelicalism's foremost defenders of biblical inerrancy and the doctrines of grace. His prolific career included numerous publications, a tenure at *Christianity Today* as a senior editor, the role of general editor for the English Standard Version of the Bible, and a faculty position at Regent College.

Packer's keen insight and articulation helped to make him one of the best and most effective popularizers of Reformed theology in the twentieth century. "What Did the Cross Achieve?" was delivered as a lecture for Tyndale House in 1973 and demonstrates Packer's theological skill as well as his ability to connect doctrine to the Christian life. His efforts shaped an entire generation of Reformed pastors and theologians who carry on the work of this modern-day Puritan.

WHAT DID THE

CROSS ACHIEVE?

THE TASK THAT I HAVE SET myself in this lecture
is to focus on and explicate a belief that, by and
large, is a distinguishing mark of the worldwide
evangelical fraternity: namely, the belief that the
cross had the character of penal substitution, and
that it was in virtue of this fact that it brought salvation to mankind. Two considerations prompt
my attempt. First, the significance of penal substitution is not always stated as exactly as is desir-
able, so that the idea often gets misunderstood and
caricatured by its critics; and I should like, if I can,
to make such misunderstanding more difficult.
Second, I am one of those who believe that this
notion takes us to the very heart of the Christian

gospel, and I welcome the opportunity of commending my conviction by analysis and argument.[1]

My plan is this: first, to clear up some questions of method, so that there will be no doubt as to what I am doing; second, to explore what it means to call Christ's death substitutionary; third, to see what further meaning is added when Christ's substitutionary suffering is called penal; fourth, to note in closing that the analysis offered is not out of harmony with learned exegetical opinion. These are, I believe, needful preliminaries to any serious theological estimate of this view.

MYSTERY AND MODEL

Every theological question has behind it a history of study, and narrow eccentricity in handling it is

---

[1] Publisher's note: Packer's original footnotes have been reduced for ease of readability.

unavoidable unless the history is taken into account. Adverse comment on the concept of penal substitution often betrays narrow eccentricity of this kind. The two main historical points relating to this idea are, first, that Luther, Calvin, Zwingli, Melanchthon, and their reforming contemporaries were the pioneers in stating it and, second, that the arguments brought against it in 1578 by the Unitarian Pelagian Faustus Socinus in his brilliant polemic *De Jesu Christo Servatore* (*Of Jesus Christ the Savior*) have been central in discussion of it ever since. What the Reformers did was redefine *satisfactio* (satisfaction), the main medieval category for thought about the cross. Anselm's *Cur Deus homo?*, which largely determined the medieval development, saw Christ's *satisfactio* for our sins as the offering of compensation or damages for dishonor done, but the Reformers saw it as the undergoing of vicarious punishment (*poena*) to meet the claims on us of God's holy law and wrath (i.e., his punitive justice). What Socinus did was to arraign this idea as irrational, incoherent, immoral, and impossible. Giving pardon, he argued, does not square with taking satisfaction, nor does the transferring of punishment from the guilty to the innocent square with justice; nor is the temporary death of one a true substitute for the eternal death of many; and a perfect substitutionary satisfaction, could such a thing be, would necessarily confer on us unlimited permission to continue in sin. Socinus's alternative account of New Testament soteriology, based on the axiom that God forgives without requiring any satisfaction save the repentance that makes us forgivable, was evasive and unconvincing, and had little influence. But his classic critique proved momentous: it held the attention of all exponents of the Reformation view for more than a century and created a tradition of rationalistic prejudice against that view, which has effectively shaped debate about it right down to our own day.

The almost mesmeric effect of Socinus's critique on Reformed scholastics in particular was on the whole unhappy. It forced them to develop rational strength in stating and connecting up the various parts of their position, which was good, but it also led them to fight back on the challenger's own ground, using the Socinian technique of arguing a priori about God as if he were a man—to be precise, a sixteenth- or seventeenth-century monarch, head of both the legislature and the judiciary in his own realm but bound nonetheless to respect existing law and judicial practice at every point. So the God of Calvary came to be presented in a whole series of expositions right down to that of Louis Berkhof (1938) as successfully avoiding all the moral and legal lapses that Socinus claimed to find in the Reformation view. But these demonstrations, however skillfully done (and demonstrators like Francis Turretin and Hodge, to name but two,[2] were very skillful indeed), had built-in weaknesses. Their stance was defensive rather than declaratory, analytical and apologetic rather than doxological and kerygmatic. They made the word of the cross sound more like a conundrum than a confession of faith—more like a puzzle, we might say, than a gospel. What was happening? Just this: that in trying to beat Socinian rationalism at its own game, Reformed theologians were conceding the Socinian assumption that every aspect of God's work of reconciliation will be exhaus-

2 Francis Turretin, *Institutio Theologiae Elenchticae Geneva* (1682), 2:xiv; A. A. Hodge, *The Atonement* (London: Nelson, 1868). Turretin's position is usefully summarized in L. W. Grensted, *A Short History of the Doctrine of the Atonement* (Manchester: Manchester University Press, 1920), 241–52.

tively explicable in terms of a natural theology of divine government drawn from the world of contemporary legal and political thought. Thus, in their zeal to show themselves rational, they became rationalistic. Here as elsewhere, methodological rationalism became in the seventeenth century a worm in the Reformed bud, leading in the next two centuries to a large-scale withering of its theological flower.

Now I do not query the substantial rightness of the Reformed view of the atonement; on the contrary, I hope to confirm it, as will appear; but I think it is vital that we should unambiguously renounce any such intellectual method as that which I have described, and look for a better one. I shall now try to commend what seems to me a sounder method by offering answers to two questions: (1) What sort of knowledge of Christ's achievement on the cross is open to us? (2) From what source and by what means do we gain it?

(1) What sort of knowledge of God's action in Christ's death may we have? That a man named Jesus was crucified under Pontius Pilate around AD 30 is common historical knowledge, but Christian beliefs about his divine identity and the significance of his dying cannot be deduced from that fact alone. What further sort of knowledge about the cross, then, may Christians enjoy?

The answer, we may say, is faith knowledge: by faith we know that God was in Christ reconciling the world to himself. Yes, indeed; but what sort of knowledge is faith knowledge? It is a kind of knowledge of which God is both giver and content. It is a Spirit-given acquaintance with divine realities, given through acquaintance with God's word. It is a kind of knowledge that makes the knower say in one and the same breath, "Whereas

I was blind, now I see" (John 9:25 KJV) and "Now we see in a mirror, dimly . . . now I know in part" (1 Cor. 13:12 NKJV). For it is a unique kind of knowledge that, though real, is not full; it is knowledge of what is discernible within a circle of light against the background of a larger darkness; it is, in short, knowledge of a mystery, the mystery of the living God at work.

"Mystery" is used here as it was by Charles Wesley when he wrote:

> 'Tis mystery all! The immortal dies!
> Who can explore his strange design?
> In vain the firstborn seraph tries
> To sound the depths of love divine![3]

"Mystery" in this sense (traditional in theology) means a reality distinct from us that in our

---

3 Publisher's note: Charles Wesley, "And Can It Be, That I Should Gain?" (1738).

very apprehending of it remains unfathomable to us: a reality that we acknowledge as actual without knowing how it is possible, and that we therefore describe as incomprehensible. Christian metaphysicians, moved by wonder at the world, speak of the created order as "imagery," meaning that there is more to it, and more of God in it, than they can grasp; and similarly Christian theologians, taught by revelation, apply the same word to the self-revealed and self-revealing God, and to his work of reconciliation and redemption through Christ. It will be seen that this definition of mystery corresponds less to Paul's use of the word *mustērion* (which he applied to the open secret of God's saving purpose, set forth in the gospel) than to his prayer that the Ephesians might "know the love of Christ which passes knowledge" (Eph. 3:19 NKJV). Knowing through divine enlightenment that which passes knowledge is precisely what it means to be acquainted with the mystery of God. The revealed "mystery" (in Paul's sense) of Christ confronts us with the unfathomable "mystery" (in the sense I defined) of the Creator who exceeds the comprehension of his creatures. Accordingly, Paul ends his full-dress, richest-ever exposition of the mystery of Christ by crying: "O depth of wealth, wisdom, and knowledge in God! How unsearchable his judgements, how untraceable his ways! Who knows the mind of the Lord? . . . Source, Guide, and Goal of all that is—to him be glory for ever! Amen" (Rom. 11:33ff. NEB). Here Paul shows, and shares, his awareness that the God of Jesus remains the God of Job, and that the highest wisdom of the theological theorist, even when working under divine inspiration as Paul did, is to recognize that he is, as it were, gazing into the sun, whose very brightness makes it impossible for him fully to see it; so that at the end of the day he has to admit that God is much more to him than theories can ever contain, and to humble himself in adoration before the one whom he can never fully analyze.

Now the atonement is a mystery in the defined sense, one aspect of the total mystery of God. But it does not stand alone in this. Every aspect of God's reality and work, without exception, is mystery. The eternal Trinity; God's sovereignty in creation, providence, and grace; the incarnation, exaltation, present reign, and approaching return of Jesus Christ; the inspiring of the Holy Scriptures; and the ministry of the Spirit in the Christian and the church—each of these (to look no further) is a reality beyond our full fathoming, just as the cross is. And theories about any of these things that used human analogies to dispel the dimension of mystery would deserve our distrust, just as rationalistic theories about the cross do.

It must be stressed that the mystery is in each case the reality itself, as distinct from anything in our apprehension of it, and as distinct therefore from our theories, problems, affirmations, and denials about it. What makes it a mystery is that creatures like ourselves can comprehend it only in part. To say this does not open the door to skepticism, for our knowledge of divine realities (like our knowledge of each other) is genuine knowledge expressed in notions that, so far as they go, are true. But it does close the door against rationalism, in the sense of theorizing that claims to explain with finality any aspect of God's way of existing and working. And with that, it alerts us to the fact that the presence in our theology of unsolved problems is not necessarily a reflection on the truth or adequacy of our thoughts.

Inadequate and untrue theories do of course exist: a theory (the word comes from the Greek term *theōrein*, meaning, "to look at") is a view or sight of something, and if one's way of looking at it is perverse one's view will be distorted, and distorted views are always full of problems. But the mere presence of problems is not enough to prove a view distorted; true views in theology also entail unsolved problems, while any view that was problem free would certainly be rationalistic and reductionist. True theories in theology, whether about the atonement or anything else, will suspect themselves of being inadequate to their object throughout. One thing that Christians know by faith is that they know only in part.

None of this, of course, is new or unfamiliar; it all belongs to the main historic stream of Christian thought. But I state it here, perhaps too laboriously, because it has not always been brought to bear rigorously enough on the doctrine of the atonement. Also, this position has linguistic implications that touch the doctrine of the atonement in ways that are not always fully grasped; and my next task is to show what these are.

Human knowledge and thoughts are expressed in words, and what we must note now is that all attempts to speak of the mystery of the unique and transcendent God involve the stretching of ordinary language. We say, for instance, that God is both plural and singular, being three in one; that he directs and determines the free acts of men; that he is wise, good, and sovereign when he allows Christians to starve or die of cancer; that the divine Son has always upheld the universe, even when he was a human baby; and so forth. At first sight, such statements might appear nonsensical (either meaningless or false). But Christians say that, though they would be nonsensical if made of men, they are true as statements about God. If so, however, it is clear that the key words are not being used in an everyday way. Whatever our views on the origins of human language and the inspiration of the Scriptures (both matters on which it seems that options are currently being broadened rather than reduced), there can be no dispute that the meaning of all the nouns, adjectives, and verbs that we use for stating facts and giving descriptions is anchored, at least in the first instance, in our experience of knowing things and people (ourselves included) in this world. Ordinary language is thus being adapted for an extraordinary purpose when we use it to speak of God. Christians have always made this adaptation easily in their prayers, praises, and proclamations, as if it were a natural thing to do (as indeed I think it is), and the doubts articulated by living (if somewhat old-fashioned) philosophers like A. J. Ayer and Antony Flew as to whether such utterance expresses knowledge and conveys information about anything more than private attitudes seem curiously provincial as well as paradoxical.[4] Moreover, it is noticeable that the common Christian verbal forms for expressing divine mysteries have from the first shown remarkable consistency and steadiness in maintaining their built-in logical strangeness, as if the apprehended reality of God was itself sustaining them (as indeed I think it was). Language about the cross illustrates this clearly: liturgies, hymns, and literature—homiletical, catechetical, and apologetic—all show that Christians have

---

4   A. J. Ayer, *Language, Truth and Logic* (London: Gollancz, 1936); Antony Flew, "Theology and Falsification," in *New Essays in Philosophical Theology*, ed. A. G. N. Flew and Alasdair MacIntyre (London: SCM, 1955), 96–130.

from the start lived by faith in Christ's death as a sacrifice made to God in reparation for their sins, however uncouth and mythological such talk sounds (and must always have sounded), however varied the presentations of atonement that teachers tried out, and however little actual theologizing about the cross went on in particular periods, especially the early centuries.

Christian language, with its peculiarities, has been much studied during the past twenty years, and two things about it have become clear. First, all its odd, stretched, contradictory, and incoherent-sounding features derive directly from the unique Christian notion of the transcendent and tripersonal Creator God. Christians regard God as free from the limits that bind creatures like ourselves, who bear God's image while not existing on his level, and Christian language, following biblical precedent, shakes free from

ordinary limits in a way that reflects this fact.
So, for instance, faced with John's declaration in
1 John 4:8–10, "God is love. . . . Herein is love, not
that we loved God, but that he loved us, and sent
his Son to be the propitiation for our sins" (KJV),
Calvin can write without hesitation: "The word
propitiation [Lat. *placatio*; Gk. *hilasmos*] has great
weight: for God, in a way that cannot be put into
words [Lat. *ineffabili quodam modo*], at the very time
when he loved us, was hostile [Lat. *infensus*] to us
till he was reconciled in Christ."[5] Calvin's phrase
"in a way that cannot be put into words" is his
acknowledgment that the mystery of God is beyond our grasp. To Calvin, this duality of attitude,
love and hostility, which in human psychologi-
cal terms is inconceivable, is part of God's moral
glory, a sentiment that might make rationalistic

5   John Calvin, *The Institutes of the Christian Religion* 2.17.

theologians shake their heads, but at which John certainly would have nodded his.

Second, Christian speech verbalizes the apprehended mystery of God by using a distinctive nonrepresentational picture language. This consists of parables, analogies, metaphors, and images piled up in balance with each other, as in the Bible itself (from which this language is first learned), and all pointing to the reality of God's presence and action in order to evoke awareness of it and response to it. Analysis of the functioning of this language is currently in full swing, and no doubt much remains to be said. Already, however, the discussion has produced one firm result of major importance—the recognition that the verbal units of Christian speech are "models," comparable to the thought models of modern physics.[6] The

6 The pioneer in stating this was Ian T. Ramsey. See his *Religious Language* (London: SCM, 1957), *Models and Mystery* (Oxford: Oxford

significance of this appears from John MacIntyre's judgment "that the theory of models succeeds in reinstating the doctrine of analogy in modern theological logic . . . and that analogy is to be interpreted in terms of a theory of models and not vice versa."[7] The doctrine of analogy is the time-harbored account, going back to Aquinas, of how ordinary language is used to speak intelligibly of a God who is partly like us (because we bear his image) and partly unlike us (because he is the infinite Creator while we are finite creatures).[8] All theological models, like the nondescriptive models of the physical sciences, have an analogical character; they are, we might say, analogies with a purpose, thought patterns that function in a

---

University Press, 1964), and *Christian Discourse* (Oxford: Oxford University Press, 1965).

7   John MacIntyre, *The Shape of Christology* (London: SCM, 1966), 63.

8   Thomas Aquinas, *Summa Theologica* 1.13. See Ian T. Ramsey, *Words about God* (London: SCM, 1971), 36ff.

particular way, teaching us to focus one area of reality (relationships with God) by conceiving of it in terms of another, better-known area of reality (relationships with each other). Thus they actually inform us about our relationship with God and through the Holy Spirit enable us to unify, clarify, and intensify our experience in that relationship.

The last song in *Joseph and the Amazing Technicolor Dreamcoat* assures us that "any dream will do" to wake the weary into joy.[9] Will any model do to give knowledge of the living God? Historically, Christians have not thought so. Their characteristic theological method, whether practiced clumsily or skillfully, consistently or inconsistently, has been to take biblical models as their God-given starting point, to base their belief system on what

9   Publisher's note: Andrew Lloyd Weber and Tim Rice, *Joseph and the Amazing Technicolor Dreamcoat* (London: Novello, 1971).

biblical writers use these models to say, and to let these models operate as controls, both suggesting and delimiting what further, secondary models may be developed in order to explicate these that are primary. As models in physics are hypotheses formed under the suggestive control of empirical evidence to correlate and predict phenomena, so Christian theological models are explanatory constructs formed to help us know, understand, and deal with God, the ultimate reality. From this standpoint, the whole study of Christian theology—biblical, historical, and systematic—is the exploring of a three-tier hierarchy of models: first, the control models given in Scripture (God, Son of God, kingdom of God, word of God, love of God, glory of God, body of Christ, justification, adoption, redemption, new birth, and so forth—in short, all the concepts analyzed in Kittel's great *Wörterbuch* and its many epigoni); next, dogmatic models that the church crystallized out to define and defend the faith (homoousion, Trinity, nature, hypostatic union, double procession, sacrament, supernatural, and others—in short, all the concepts usually dealt with in doctrinal textbooks); finally, interpretive models lying between Scripture and defined dogma that particular theologians and theological schools developed for stating the faith to contemporaries (penal substitution, verbal inspiration, divinization, Barth's *nihil*—*das Nichtige*—and many more).

It is helpful to think of theology in these terms, and of the atonement in particular. Socinus went wrong in this matter first by identifying the biblical model of God's kingship with his own sixteenth-century monarchy model (a mistake later repeated by Hugo Grotius), second by treating this not-wholly-biblical model as his control, and third by failing to acknowledge that the mystery of God is more than any one model, even the best, can express. We have already noticed that some orthodox writers answering Socinus tended to slip in a similar way. The passion to pack God into a conceptual box of our own making is always strong, but must be resisted. If we bear in mind that all the knowledge we can have of the atonement is of a mystery about which we can only think and speak by means of models, and that remains a mystery when all is said and done, it will keep us from rationalistic pitfalls and thus help our progress considerably.

BIBLE AND MODEL

(2) Now we come up to our second question, my answer to which has been hinted at already. By what means is knowledge of the mystery of the cross given us? I reply: through the didactic

thought models given in the Bible, which in truth are instruction from God. In other words, I proceed on the basis of the mainstream Christian belief in biblical inspiration, which I have sought to justify elsewhere.

What this belief means, in formula terms, is that the Holy Scriptures of both Testaments have the dual character that the viva voce teaching of prophets, apostles, and supremely Jesus had: in content, if not in grammatical form, it is both human witness to God and God's witness to himself. The true analogy for inspiration is incarnation, the personal Word of God becoming flesh. As a multiple confession of faith in the God who rules, judges, and saves in the space-time continuum that we call world history, the Bible consists of occasional documents—historical, didactic, and liturgical—all proclaiming in various ways what God has done, is doing, and will do.

Each document and each utterance within that document, like Jesus Christ and each of his utterances, is anchored in a particular historical situation—this particularity marks all the Christian revelation—and to discern within these particularities truths from God for universal application is the interpreter's major task. His guideline is the knowledge that God's word for today is found through understanding and reapplying the word that God spoke long ago in identity (substantial, not grammatical) with the message of the biblical authors. The way into God's mind remains via their minds, for their assertions about God embody in particularized form what he wants to tell us today about himself. In other words, God says in application to us the same things that he originally said in application to those to whom the biblical books were first addressed. The details of the second application differ from the first in a way that corresponds to the difference between our situation and that of the first addressees, but the truths of principle being applied are the same. Divine speech is itself, of course, a model, but it is a controlling one. It signifies the reality of mind-to-mind instruction from God to us by verbal means, and thus teaches us to categorize all other didactic models found in Scripture, not as hypothesis or hunch, but as revelation.

How do these revealed models become means of God's instruction? Here, it must regretfully be said, Ian Ramsey, the pioneer exponent of the model structure of biblical thinking, fails us. He describes vividly how these models trigger off religious "disclosures" and so evoke religious responses, but instead of equating the beliefs they express with divine teaching, he leaves quite open, and therefore quite obscure, the relation between the "disclosures" as intuitions of reality and the thoughts that the models convey. This means that he lacks criteria for distinguishing true from false intuitions. Sometimes he speaks as if all feelings of "cosmic disclosure" convey insights that are true and self-authenticating, but one need only mention the Buddha, Mohammed, Mary Baker Eddy, the fake prophets exposed by Jeremiah, Ezekiel, and Micaiah in 1 Kings 22, and the visionaries of Colossians 2:18 to show that this is not so. Also Ramsey seems to be without criteria for relating models to each other and developing from them a coherent belief system, and he nowhere considers what the divine-speech model implies.

Must our understanding of how biblical models function be as limited or as loose as Ramsey's is? Not necessarily. Recognition that the biblical witness to God has the logic of models—not isolated, incidentally, but linked together, and qualifying each other in sizeable units of meaning—is compatible with all the views taken in the modern hermeneutical debate. Central to this debate are two questions. The first is whether the reference point and subject matter of biblical witness is just the transformed psyche, the "new being" as such, or whether it does not also, and indeed primarily, refer to saving acts of God and a living divine Savior that were originally there as datable realities in the space-time continuum of world history, and that owe their transforming power "here" in Christian lives now to the fact that they were "there" on the stage of history then. To the extent that the former alternative is embraced, one has to say that the only factual information that the biblical writers communicate is that God's people felt and thought in certain ways at certain times in certain situations. Then one has to face the question of whether the writers thought this was all the factual information they were communicating; if one says no, then one has to justify one's disagreement with them; if one says yes, one has to explain why so much of their witness to Christ has the form of factual narration about him—why, indeed, the gospel as a literary form was ever invented. If, however, one takes the latter alternative, as all sober reason seems to counsel, then the second central question arises: how much distortion of fact is there in the narrating, and how much of guesswork, hunch, and fantasy is there in the interpreting of the historical realities that were "there"? I cannot discuss these massive and complex issues here; suffice it to declare, in relation to this debate, that I am proceeding on the basis that the biblical writers do indeed give true information about certain historical events, public and in principle datable, which have resulted in a Savior and a salvation being "there" for sinners to receive by faith; and that the biblical thought models in terms of which these events are presented and explained are revealed models, ways of thought that God himself has taught us for the true understanding of what he has done for us and will do in us.

Also, I proceed on the basis that the Holy Spirit who inspired prophetic and apostolic testimony in its written as well as its oral form is now active to teach Christians through it, making them aware of its divine quality overall, its message to themselves, and the presence and potency of God in Christ to whom it points. Since the Spirit has been teaching the church in this way in every age, much of our listening to the Bible in the present will rightly take the form of reviewing theological constructions of the past, testing them by the written word from which they took their rise. When a particular theological view, professedly

Bible based, has over the centuries proved a main-spring of Christian devotion, faith, and love, one approaches it, not indeed uncritically, but with respect, anticipating the discovery that it is substantially right. Our present task is to elucidate and evaluate one historic line of biblical interpretation that has had an incalculable impact on countless lives since it was clarified in the century of the Reformation; it will be strange if it proves to have been entirely wrong.

So much, then, for methodological preliminaries, which have been tedious but necessary; now to our theme directly.

SUBSTITUTION

The first thing to say about penal substitution has been said already. It is a Christian theological model, based on biblical exegesis, formed to focus a particular awareness of what Jesus did at Calvary to bring us to God. If we wish to speak of the *doctrine* of penal substitution, we should remember that this model is a dramatic, kerygmatic picturing of divine action, much more like Aulén's classic idea of divine victory (though Aulén never saw this) than it is like the defensive formula models that we call the Nicene doctrine of the Trinity and the Chalcedonian doctrine of the person of Christ. Logically, the model is put together in two stages: first, the death of Christ is declared to have been substitutionary; then the substitution is characterized, and given a specific frame of reference by adding the word "penal." We shall examine the two stages separately.

Stage one is to declare Christ's death substitutionary. What does this mean? The *Oxford English Dictionary* defines substitution as "the putting of one person or thing in the place of another."[10] One oddity of contemporary Christian talk is that many who affirm that Jesus's death was vicarious and representative deny that it was substitutionary; for the dictionary defines both words in substitutionary terms! "Representation" is said to mean "the fact of standing for, or in place of, some other thing or person, esp. with a right or authority to act on their account; substitution of one thing or person for another."[11] And "vicarious" is defined as something or someone "that takes or supplies the place of another thing or person; substituted instead of the proper thing or person."[12] So here, it seems, is a distinction without a difference. Substitution is, in fact, a broad idea that applies

---

10 Publisher's note: *Oxford English Dictionary,* s.v. "substitution."
11 Publisher's note: Packer seems to be quoting the OED.
12 Publisher's note: Packer seems to be quoting the OED.

whenever one person acts to supply another's need, or to discharge his obligation, so that the other no longer has to carry the load himself. As Pannenberg says, "in social life, substitution is a universal phenomenon. . . . Even the structure of vocation, the division of labour, has substitutionary character. One who has a vocation performs this function for those whom he serves," for "every service has vicarious character by recognizing a need in the person served that apart from the service that person would have to satisfy for himself."[13] In this broad sense, nobody who wishes to say with Paul that there is a true sense in which "Christ died for us" (*huper*, meaning, "on our behalf; for our benefit"), and "Christ has redeemed us from the curse of the law, having become a curse for us" (*huper* again; Rom. 5:8;

13 Wolfhart Pannenberg, *Jesus: God and Man*, trans. Lewis L. Wilkins and Duane A. Priebe (London: SCM, 1968), 268, 259.

Gal. 3:13 NKJV), and who accepts Christ's assurance that he came "to give his life a ransom for many" (*anti*, which means precisely "in place of; in exchange for"), should hesitate to say that Christ's death was substitutionary. Indeed, if he describes Christ's death as vicarious he is actually saying it.

It is, of course, no secret why people shy off this word. It is because they equate, and know that others equate, substitution in Christology with penal substitution. This explains the state of affairs that, writing in 1948, F. W. Camfield described as follows:

> If there is one conclusion which [has] come almost to be taken for granted in enlightened Christian quarters, it is that the idea of substitution has led theology on a wrong track; and that the word "substitution" must now be

dropped from the doctrine of the Atonement as too heavily laden with misleading and even false connotations. By "liberal" or "modernist" theology the idea of substitution is of course rejected out of hand. And even the theology which prides itself on being "positive" and "evangelical" and which seeks to maintain lines of communication with the great traditional doctrines of atonement is on the whole disposed to reject it. And this, not merely on the ground that it holds implications which are irrational and morally offensive, but even and specifically on the ground that it is unscriptural. Thus Dr. Vincent Taylor as a result of exhaustive examination of the "Idea of Atonement in the New Testament" gives it as his conclusion that the idea of substitution has no place in the New Testament writings; that in fact it is opposed to the fundamental teaching of the New Testament; that even St Paul though he sometimes trembles on the edge of substitutionary conceptions nevertheless avoids them. It is difficult to escape the impression that Dr. Vincent Taylor's anxiety to eliminate the idea of substitution from evangelical theology has coloured his interpretation of the New Testament witness. But his conclusions provide a striking indication of the tendency at work in modern evangelical circles. It is felt that nothing has done more to bring the evangelical doctrine of the Atonement into disrepute than the idea of substitution; and therefore, something like a sigh of relief makes itself heard when it is suggested that this idea rests on a misunderstanding of the teaching of Scripture.[14]

14 F. W. Camfield, "The Idea of Substitution in the Doctrine of the Atonement," *Scottish Journal of Theology* 1 (1948): 282f. See Vincent

Today, more than a quarter of a century later, the picture Camfield draws would have to be qualified by reference to the vigorous vindication and use of the substitution idea by such as Pannenberg and Barth;[15] nonetheless, in British theology the overall situation remains very much as Camfield describes. It would, however, clarify discussion if all who hold that Jesus by dying did something for us that we needed to do but could not, would agree that they are regarding Christ's death as substitutionary, and differing only on the nature of the action that Jesus performed in our place, and also, perhaps, on the way we enter into the benefit that flows from it. Camfield himself goes on to spell out a nonpenal view of substitution.

Taylor, *The Atonement in New Testament Teaching* (London: Epworth, 1963).

15 Pannenberg, *Jesus*, 258–69; Karl Barth, *Church Dogmatics*, trans. G. W. Bromiley (Edinburgh: T&T Clark, 1956), 4:viif., 230ff., 550ff.

Broadly speaking, there have been three ways in which Christ's death has been explained in the church. Each reflects a particular view of the nature of God and our plight in sin, and of what is needed to bring us to God in the fellowship of acceptance on his side and faith and love on ours. It is worth glancing at them to see how the idea of substitution fits in with each.

There is first the type of account that sees the cross as having its effect entirely on men, whether by revealing God's love to us, or by bringing home to us how much God hates our sins, or by setting us a supreme example of godliness, or by blazing a trail to God that we may now follow, or by so involving mankind in his redemptive obedience that the life of God now flows into us, or by all these modes together. It is assumed that our basic need is lack of motivation Godward and of openness to the inflow of divine life; all that is needed to set us in a right relationship with God is a change in us at these two points, and this Christ's death brings about. The forgiveness of our sins is not a separate problem; as soon as we are changed we become forgivable, and are then forgiven at once. This view has little or no room for any thought of substitution, since it goes so far in equating what Christ did for us with what he does to us.

A second type of account sees Christ's death as having its effect primarily on hostile spiritual forces external to us that are held to be imprisoning us in a captivity of which our inveterate moral twistedness is one sign and symptom. The cross is seen as the work of God going forth to battle as our champion, just as David went forth as Israel's champion to fight Goliath. Through the cross these hostile forces, however conceived—whether as sin and death,

Satan and his hosts, the demonic in society and its structures, the powers of God's wrath and curse, or anything else—are overcome and nullified, so that Christians are not in bondage to them but share Christ's triumph over them. The assumption here is that man's plight is created entirely by hostile cosmic forces distinct from God; yet, seeing Jesus as our champion, exponents of this view could still properly call him our substitute, just as all the Israelites who declined Goliath's challenge in 1 Samuel 17:8–11 could properly call David their substitute. Just as a substitute who involves others in the consequences of his action as if they had done it themselves is their representative, so a representative discharging the obligations of those whom he represents is their substitute. What this type of account of the cross affirms (though it is not usually put in these terms) is that the conquering Christ, whose victory secured our release, was our representative substitute.

The third type of account denies nothing asserted by the other two views save their assumption that they are complete. There is biblical support for all they say, but it goes further. It grounds man's plight as a victim of sin and Satan in the fact that, for all God's daily goodness to him, as a sinner he stands under divine judgment, and his bondage to evil is the start of his sentence, and unless God's rejection of him is turned into acceptance he is lost forever. On this view, Christ's death had its effect first on God, who was hereby propitiated (or better, who hereby propitiated himself), and only because it had this effect did it become an overthrowing of the powers of darkness and a revealing of God's seeking and saving love. The thought here is that by dying, Christ offered to God what the West has called satisfaction for sins, satisfaction that God's own character dictated as the only means whereby his "no" to us could become a "yes." Whether this Godward satisfaction is understood as the homage of death itself, or death as the perfecting of holy obedience, or an undergoing of the Godforsakenness of hell, which is God's final judgment on sin, or a perfect confession of man's sins combined with entry into their bitterness by sympathetic identification, or all these things together (and nothing stops us combining them together), the shape of this view remains the same—that by undergoing the cross Jesus expiated our sins, propitiated our Maker, turned God's "no" to us into a "yes," and so saved us. All forms of this view see Jesus as our representative substitute in fact, whether or not they call him that, but only certain versions of it represent his substitution as penal.

This analysis prompts three comments.

First, it should be noted that though the two former views regularly set themselves in antithesis to the third, the third takes up into itself all the positive assertions that they make. This raises the question whether any more is at issue here than the impropriety of treating half-truth as the whole truth and of rejecting a more comprehensive account on the basis of speculative negations about what God's holiness requires as a basis for forgiving sins. Were it allowed that the first two views might be misunderstanding and distorting themselves in this way, the much-disputed claim that a broadly substitutionary view of the cross has always been the mainstream Christian opinion might be seen to have substance in it after all. It is a pity that books on the atonement so often take it for granted that accounts of the cross that have appeared as rivals in historical debate must be treated as intrinsically exclusive. This is always arbitrary, and sometimes quite perverse.

Second, it should be noted that our analysis was simply of views about the death of Christ, so nothing was said about his resurrection. All three types of view usually agree in affirming that the resurrection is an integral part of the gospel. That the gospel proclaims a living, vindicated Savior whose resurrection as the firstfruits of the new humanity is the basis as well as the pattern for ours is not a matter of dispute between them. It is sometimes pointed out that the second view represents the resurrection of Jesus as an organic element in his victory over the powers of death, whereas the third view does not, and hardly could, represent it as an organic element in the bearing of sin's penalty or the tasting and confessing of its vileness (however the work of Calvary is conceived); and on this basis the third view is sometimes criticized as making the resurrection unnecessary. But this criticism may be met in two ways. The first reply is that Christ's saving work has two parts—his dealing with his Father on our behalf by offering himself in substitutionary satisfaction for our sins and his dealing with us on his Father's behalf by bestowing on us through faith the forgiveness that his death secured—and it is as important to distinguish these two parts as it is to hold them together. For a demonstration that part two is now possible because part one is finished, and for the actual implementing of part two, Jesus's resurrection is indeed essential, and so appears as an organic element in his work as a whole. The second reply is that these two ways of viewing the cross should in any case be synthesized, following the example of Paul in Colossians 2:13–15, as being complementary models expressing different elements in the single complex reality that is the mystery of the cross.

Third, it should be noted that not all advocates of the third type of view have been happy to use the word "substitution." This has been partly through desire to evade the Socinian criticism that in the penal realm substitution is impossible, and partly for fear that to think of Christ dying for us as our substitute obscures his call to us to die and rise in him and with him for the moral transforming of us into his holy image. P. T. Forsyth, for example, is one who stresses the vicariousness of Christ's action in his passion as he endured for man's salvation God's personal anger against man's sin.[16] Yet he rejects substitution in favor

---

16 "He turned the penalty He endured into sacrifice He offered. And the sacrifice He offered was the judgment He accepted. His passive suffering became active obedience, and obedience to a holy doom." P. T. Forsyth, *The Work of Christ* (London: Hodder and Stoughton, 1910), 163.

of representation and replaces "substitutionary expiation" (which, as these words are commonly understood, leaves us too little committed) with "solidary reparation" and "solidary confession and praise" because he wants to stress that we enter into salvation only as we identify with Christ's death to sin and are recreated as the new humanity in him.[17] But, admirable as is Forsyth's wish to stress what is in Romans 6:1–11, avoiding the word "substitution" can only have the effect of obscuring what is in Romans 3:21–28, where Paul describes Christ as "a propitiation by his blood" (3:25) in virtue of which God bestows "the free gift of righteousness" (5:17) upon believing sinners and so "justifies the ungodly" (4:5). As James Denney said, "If Christ died the death in which sin had involved us—if in His death He took the

17   Forsyth, *Work of Christ*, 164, 182, 223, 225f. "Substitution does not take account of the moral results [of the cross] on the soul" (182).

responsibility of our sins on Himself—no word is equal to this which falls short of what is meant by calling Him our substitute."[18] The correct reply to Forsyth would seem to be that before Christ's death can be representative (in Forsyth's sense of setting a pattern of "confession and praise" to be reproduced in our own self-denial and cross bearing) it has to be substitutionary in Denney's sense of absorbing God's wrath against our sins. Otherwise, our "confession and praise" in solidarity with Christ becomes itself a ploy for averting that wrath—in other words, a meritorious work, aimed at securing pardon, assuming that in Christ we save ourselves.

What Denney said about this in 1903 was in fact an answer in anticipation of Forsyth's formula of 1910. A reviewer of *The Death of Christ* had argued

18 James Denney, *The Death of Christ*, 2nd ed. (London: Hodder and Stoughtons, 1911), 73.

that "if we place ourselves at Paul's point of view, we shall see that to the eye of God the death of Christ presents itself less as an act which Christ does for the race than as an act which the race does in Christ."[19] In *The Atonement and the Modern Mind*, Denney quoted these words and commented on them thus:

> In plain English, Paul teaches less that Christ died for the ungodly, than that the ungodly in Christ died for themselves. This brings out the logic of what representative means when representative is opposed to substitute. The representative is ours, we are in Him, and we are supposed to get over all the moral difficulties raised by the idea of substitution just because He is ours, and because we are one with Him. But the fundamental fact of

19 Publisher's note: See Denney, *Death of Christ*, chap. 9.

54

the situation is that, to begin with, Christ is not ours, and we are not one with Him. . . . we are "without Christ" (*choris Christou*). . . . A representative not produced by us, but given to us—not chosen by us, but the elect of God—is not a representative at all in the first instance, but a substitute.[20]

So the true position, on the type of view we are exploring, may be put thus: We identify with Christ against the practice of sin because we have already identified him as the one who took our place under sentence for sin. We enter upon the life of repentance because we have learned that he first endured for us the death of reparation. The Christ into whom we now accept incorporation is the Christ who previously on the cross became our propitiation—not, therefore, one in

20   Denney, *Death of Christ*, 304.

whom we achieve our reconciliation with God, but one through whom we receive it as a free gift based on a finished work (Rom. 5:10); and we love him, because he first loved us and gave himself for us. So substitution, on this view, really is the basic category; the thought of Christ as our representative, however construed in detail, cannot be made to mean what substitution means, and our solidarity with Christ in "confession and praise," so far from being a concept alternative to that of substitution, is actually a response that presupposes it.

PENAL SUBSTITUTION

Now we move to the second stage in our model building, and bring in the word "penal" to characterize the substitution we have in view. To add this "qualifier," as Ramsey would call it, is to anchor the model of substitution (not exclusively, but regulatively) within the world of moral law, guilty conscience, and retributive justice. Thus is forged a conceptual instrument for conveying the thought that God remits our sins and accepts our persons into favor not because of any amends we have attempted, but because the penalty that was our due was diverted onto Christ. The notion that the phrase "penal substitution" expresses is that Jesus Christ our Lord, moved by a love that was determined to do everything necessary to save us, endured and exhausted the destructive divine judgment for which we were otherwise inescapably destined, and so won us forgiveness, adoption, and glory. To affirm penal substitution is to say that believers are in debt to Christ specifically for this, and that this is the mainspring of all their joy, peace, and praise both now and for eternity.

The general thought is clear enough, but for our present purpose we need a fuller analysis of its meaning, and here a methodological choice must be made. Should we appeal to particular existing accounts of penal substitution or construct a composite of our own? At the risk of seeming idiosyncratic (which is, I suppose, the gentleman's way of saying unsound) I plump for the latter course, for the following main reasons.

First, there is no denying that penal substitution sometimes has been, and still sometimes is, asserted in ways that merit the favorite adjective of its critics—"crude." As one would expect of that which for more than four centuries has been the mainspring of evangelical piety ("popular piety," as Roman Catholics would call it), ways of presenting it have grown up that are devotionally evocative without always being theologically rigorous. Moreover, the more theological expositions of it since Socinus have tended to be one-track minded. Constricted in interest by the preoccupations of controversy, and absorbed in the task of proclaiming the one vital truth about the cross that others disregarded or denied, "upholders of the penal theory have sometimes so stressed the thought that Christ bore our penalty that they have found room for nothing else. Rarely have they in theory denied the value of other theories, but sometimes they have in practice ignored them."[21] Also, as we have seen, much of the more formative and influential discussions of penal substitution were held in the seventeenth century, at a time when Protestant exegesis of Scripture was colored by an uncriticized and indeed unrecognized natural

21 Leon Morris, *The Cross in the New Testament* (Exeter: Paternoster, 1965), 401.

theology of law, and this has left its mark on many later statements. All this being so, it might be hard to find an account of penal substitution that could safely be taken as standard or as fully representative, and it will certainly be more straightforward if I venture an analysis of my own.

Second, I have already hinted that I think it important for the theory of penal substitution to be evaluated as a model setting forth the meaning of the atonement rather than its mechanics. One result of the work of rationalistic Protestant theologians over three centuries, from the Socinians to the Hegelians, was to nourish the now common assumption that the logical function of a theory in theology is to resolve "how" problems within an established frame of thought about God and man. In other words, theological theories are like detectives' theories in whodunits;

they are hypotheses relating puzzling facts together in such a way that all puzzlement is dispelled (for the convention of mystery stories is that by the last page no mystery should be felt to remain). Now we have seen that, for discernible historical reasons, penal substitution has sometimes been explicated as a theory of this kind, telling us how divine love and justice could be, and were, "reconciled" (whatever that means); but a doubt remains as to whether this way of understanding the theme is biblically right. Is the harmonization of God's attributes any part of the information, or is it even the kind of information, that the inspired writers are concerned to give? Gustaf Aulén characterized the *Christus victor* motif (he would not call it a theory) as a dramatic idea of the atonement rather than a rationale of its mechanics, and contrasted it in this respect with the "Latin" view, of which penal substitution is one form;[22] but should not penal substitution equally be understood as a dramatic idea, declaring the fact of the atonement kerygmatically, that is, as gospel (good news), just as Aulén's conquest motif is concerned to do? I believe it should. Surely the primary issue with which penal substitution is concerned is neither the morality nor the rationality of God's ways but the remission of my sins. And the primary function of the concept is to correlate my knowledge of being guilty before God with my knowledge that, on the one hand, no question of my ever being judged for my sins can now arise, and, on the other hand, that the risen Christ whom I am called to accept as Lord is none other than Jesus, who secured my immunity from judgment by bearing on the cross the penalty that was my due.

22   Gustaf Aulén, *Christus Victor* (London: 1931), 175.

The effect of this correlation is not in any sense to "solve" or dissipate the mystery of the work of God (it is not that sort of mystery!); the effect is simply to define that work with precision, and thus to evoke faith, hope, praise, and responsive love to Jesus Christ. So, at least, I think, and therefore I wish my presentation of penal substitution to highlight its character as a kerygmatic model. And so I think it best to offer my own analytical definition, which will aim to be both descriptive of what all who have held this view have had in common, and also prescriptive of how the term should be understood in any future discussion.

Third, if the present examination of penal substitution is to be worthwhile it must present this view in its best light, and I think an eclectic exposition will bring us closest to this goal. The typical modern criticism of older expositions of our theme is that, over and above their being less than fully moral (Socinus's criticism), they are less than fully personal. Thus, for instance, G. W. H. Lampe rejects penal substitution because it assumes that "God inflicts retributive punishment," and

> retribution is impersonal; it considers offences in the abstract . . . we ought not to ascribe purely retributive justice to God . . . the Father of mankind does not deal with his children on the basis of deterrence and retribution . . . to hang the criminal is to admit defeat at the level of love. . . . It is high time to discard the vestiges of a theory of Atonement that was geared to a conception of punishment which found nothing shocking in the idea that God should crucify sinners or the substitute who took their place. It is time, too, to stop the mouth of the blasphemer who

calls it "sentimentality" to reject the idea of a God of retribution.[23]

Lampe's violent language shows the strength of his conviction that retribution belongs to a subpersonal, nonloving order of relationships, and that penal substitution dishonors the cross by anchoring it here.

James Denney's sense of the contrast between personal relations, which are moral, and legal relations, which tend to be impersonal, external, and arbitrary, once drew from him an outburst that in isolation might seem parallel to Lampe's. "Few things have astonished me more," he wrote,

than to be charged with teaching a "forensic" or "legal" or "judicial" doctrine

23 G. W. H. Lampe, "The Atonement: Law and Love," in *Soundings*, ed. A. R. Vidler (Cambridge: Cambridge University Press, 1962), 187ff.

of Atonement. . . . There is nothing that I should wish to reprobate more whole-heartedly than the conception which is expressed by these words. To say that the relations of God and man are forensic is to say that they are regulated by statute—that sin is a breach of statute—that the sinner is a criminal—and that God adjudicates on him by interpreting the statute in its application to his case. Everybody knows that this is a travesty of the truth.[24]

It is noticeable that Denney, the champion of the substitutionary idea, never calls Christ's sub-stitution "penal"; in his situation, the avoidance must have been deliberate. Yet Denney affirmed these four truths: first, that "the relations of God and man . . . are personal, but . . . determined by

24 Denney, *Death of Christ*, 271f.

[moral] law"; second, "that there is in the nature of things a reaction against sin which when it has had its perfect work is fatal, that this reaction is the divine punishment of sin, and that its finally fatal character is what is meant by Scripture when it says that the wages of sin is death"; third, that "the inevitable reactions of the divine order against evil . . . are the sin itself coming back in another form and finding out the sinner. They are nothing if not retributive"; and, fourth,

> that while the agony and the Passion were not penal in the sense of coming upon Jesus through a bad conscience, or making Him the personal object of divine wrath, they were penal in the sense that in that dark hour He had to realise to the full the divine reaction against sin in the race . . . and that without

doing so He could not have been the Redeemer of that race from sin.[25]

It seems to me that these affirmations point straight to a way of formulating the penal substitution model that is both moral and personal enough to evade all Lampe's strictures and also inclusive of all that the concept means to those who embrace it. But the formulation itself will have to be my own.

So I shall now attempt my analysis of penal substitution as a model of the atonement, under five heads: (1) substitution and retribution, (2) substitution and solidarity, (3) substitution and mystery, (4) substitution and salvation, and (5) substitution and divine love. Others who espouse this model must judge whether I analyze it accurately or not.

25 James Denney, *The Christian Doctrine of Reconciliation* (London: Hodder and Stoughton, 1917), 187, 214, 208, 273.

Substitution and Retribution

Penal substitution, as an idea, presupposes a penalty (*poena*) due to us from God the Judge for wrong done and failure to meet his claims. The *locus classicus* on this is Romans 1:18–3:20; but the thought is everywhere in the New Testament. The judicial context is a moral context, too; whereas human judicial systems are not always rooted in moral reality, the Bible treats the worlds of moral reality and of divine judgment as coinciding. Divine judgment means that retribution is entailed by our past upon our present and future existence, and God himself is in charge of this process, ensuring that the objective wrongness and guiltiness of what we have been is always "there" to touch and wither what we are and shall be. In the words of Emil Brunner, "Guilt means that our past—that which can never be made good—always constitutes one element in our present situation."[26] When Lady Macbeth, walking and talking in her sleep, sees blood on her hand and cannot clean or sweeten it, she witnesses to the order of retribution as all writers of tragedy and surely all reflective men—certainly, those who believe in penal substitution—have come to know it: wrongdoing may be forgotten for a time, as David forgot his sin over Bathsheba and Uriah, but sooner or later it comes back to mind, as David's sin did under Nathan's ministry, and at once our attention is absorbed, our peace and pleasure are gone, and something tells us that we ought to suffer for what we have done. When joined with inklings of God's displeasure, this sense of things is the start of hell. Now it is into this context of awareness that the model of

26 Emil Brunner, *The Mediator*, trans. O. Wyon (London: Lutterworth, 1934), 443.

penal substitution is introduced, to focus for us four insights about our situation.

Insight one concerns God: it is that the retributive principle has his sanction, and indeed expresses the holiness, justice, and goodness reflected in his law, and that death—spiritual as well as physical, the loss of the life of God as well as that of the body—is the rightful sentence that he has announced against us and now prepares to inflict.

Insight two concerns ourselves: it is that, standing thus under sentence, we are helpless either to undo the past or to shake off sin in the present, and thus have no way of averting what threatens.

Insight three concerns Jesus Christ: it is that he, the God-man of John 1:1–18 and Hebrews 1–2, took our place under judgment and received in his own personal experience all the dimensions of the death that was our sentence, whatever these were, so laying the foundation for our pardon and immunity:

> We may not know, we cannot tell
> What pains he had to bear;
> But we believe it was for us
> He hung and suffered there.[27]

Insight four concerns faith: it is that faith is a matter first and foremost of looking outside and away from oneself to Christ and his cross as the sole ground of present forgiveness and future hope. Faith sees that God's demands remain what they were and that God's law of retribution, which our conscience declares to be right, has not ceased to operate in his world nor ever will, but that in our case the law has operated

---

27   Publisher's note: Cecil Frances Alexander, "There is a Green Hill Far Away" (1848).

already, so that all our sins—past, present, and even future—have been covered by Calvary. So our conscience is pacified by the knowledge that our sins have already been judged and punished, however strange the statement may sound, in the person and death of another. Bunyan's pilgrim before the cross loses his burden, and Toplady can assure himself that

> If thou my pardon hast secured,
> And freely in my room endured
> The whole of wrath divine,
> Payment God cannot twice demand,
> First from my bleeding surety's hand
> And then again from mine.[28]

Reasoning thus, faith grasps the reality of God's free gift of righteousness, that is, the rightness

28 Publisher's note: Augustus Toplady, "Faith Reviving" (n.d.).

with God that the righteous enjoy (Rom. 5:16f.), and with it the justified man's obligation to live henceforth "unto" the one who for his sake died and rose again (2 Cor. 5:15).

This analysis, if correct, shows what job the word "penal" does in our model. It is there not to prompt theoretical puzzlement about the transferring of guilt but to articulate the insight of believers who, as they look at Calvary in the light of the New Testament, are constrained to say, "Jesus was bearing the judgment I deserved (and deserve), the penalty for my sins, the punishment due to me"—he "loved me, and gave himself for me" (Gal. 2:20 KJV). How it was possible for him to bear their penalty they do not claim to know, any more than they know how it was possible for him to be made man; but that he bore it is the certainty on which all their hopes rest.

Substitution and Solidarity

Anticipating the rationalistic criticism that guilt is not transferable and that the substitution described, if real, would be immoral, our model now invokes Paul's description of the Lord Jesus Christ as the second man and last Adam, who involved us in his sin bearing as truly as Adam involved us in his sinning (1 Cor. 15:45ff.; Rom. 5:12ff.). Penal substitution was seen by Luther (the pioneer in stating it), and by those who came after, as grounded in this ontological solidarity and as being one moment in the larger mystery of what Luther called "a wonderful exchange"[29] and Morna Hooker designates "interchange in Christ."[30] In this mystery

---

29 Martin Luther, D. *Martin Luther's Werke* (Weimar: H. Böhlau, 1883), 5:608.
30 Morna Hooker, "Interchange in Christ," *Journal of Theological Studies* 22 (1971): 349–361.

there are four moments to be distinguished. The first is the incarnation when the Son of God came into the human situation, "born of a woman, born under the law, that he might redeem them that were under the law" (Gal. 4:4f. ASV). The second moment was the cross, where Jesus, as Luther and Calvin put it, carried our identity[31] and effectively involved us all in his dying—as Paul says, "One died for all, therefore all died" (2 Cor. 5:14 NASB). This sharing in Christ's death is not a legal fiction, a form of words to which no reality corresponds; it is part of the objective fact of Christ, the mystery that is "there" whether we grasp it or not. So now Christ's substitution for us, which is exclusive in the sense of making the work of atonement wholly his and allowing us no share in performing it, is seen to be from another

31 Martin Luther, *Galatians*, ed. Philip S. Watson (London: James Clarke, 1953), 269–271; Calvin, *Institutes* 2.17.

standpoint inclusive of us, inasmuch as ontologically and objectively, in a manner transcending bounds of space and time, Christ has taken us with him into his death and through his death into his resurrection. Thus, knowledge of Christ's death for us as our sin-bearing substitute requires us to see ourselves as dead, risen, and alive forevermore in him. We who believe have died—painlessly and invisibly, we might say—in solidarity with him because he died, painfully and publicly, in substitution for us. His death for us brought remission of sins committed in Adam so that in him we might enjoy God's acceptance; our death in him brings release from the existence we knew in Adam, so that in him we are raised to new life and become new creatures (Rom. 5–6; 2 Cor. 5:17, 21; Col. 2:6–3:4). The third moment in this interchange comes when, through faith and God's gift of the Spirit, we become "the righteousness of God" and "rich"—that is, justified from sin and accepted as heirs of God in and with Christ—by virtue of him who became "poor" for us in the incarnation and was "made . . . sin" for us by penal substitution on the cross (2 Cor. 8:9; 5:21). And the fourth moment will be when this same Jesus Christ, who was exalted to glory after being humbled to death for us (Phil. 2:5–11), reappears to "fashion anew the body of our humiliation, that it may be conformed to the body of his glory" (Phil. 3:21 ASV).

Sometimes it is urged that in relation to this comprehensive mystery of solidarity and interchange, viewed as a whole, Christ the "pioneer" (*archēgos*; Heb. 2:10; 12:2) is best designated the "representative" and "firstfruits" of the new humanity rather than our "substitute."[32] Inasmuch

---

32 For "representative" see Hooker, "Interchange in Christ," 358; G. W. H. Lampe, *Reconciliation in Christ* (London: Longmans, 1956),

as the interchange theme centers upon our renewal in Christ's image, this point may be readily
accepted, provided it is also seen that in relation
to the particular mystery of sin bearing, which is
at the heart of the interchange, Christ as victim
of the penal process has to be called our substitute, since the purpose and effect of his suffering
was precisely to ensure that no such suffering—
no Godforsakenness, no dereliction—should
remain for us. In the light of earlier discussion,
we are already entitled to dismiss the proposal
to call Christ's death representative rather than
substitutionary as both confusing and confused
since it suggests, first, that we chose Christ to act
for us, second, that the death we die in him is of
the same order as the death he died for us, and
third, that by dying in Christ we atone for our

---

chap. 3. For "firstfruits," see D. F. H. Whiteley, *The Theology of
St. Paul* (Oxford: Blackwell, 1964), 132ff.

sins—all of which are false. Here now is a further reason for rejecting the proposal—namely, that it misses or muffs the point that what Christ bore on the cross was the Godforsakenness of penal judgment, which we shall never have to bear because he accepted it in our place. The appropriate formulation is that on the cross Jesus's representative relation to us, as the last Adam whose image we are to bear, took the form of substituting for us under judgment, as the suffering servant of God on whom the Lord "laid . . . the iniquity of us all" (Isa. 53:6). The two ideas, representation and substitution, are complementary, not alternatives, and both are needed here.

Substitution and Mystery

It will by now be clear that those who affirm penal substitution offer this model not as an explanatory analysis of what lay behind Christ's atoning death (in the way that the laws of heat provide an explanatory analysis of what lies behind the boiling of a kettle), but rather as a pointer directing attention to various fundamental features of the mystery—that is, according to our earlier definition, the transcendent and not-wholly-comprehensible divine reality—of Christ's atoning death itself, as the New Testament writers declare it. Most prominent among these features are the mysterious divine love that was its source, and of which it is the measure (Rom. 5:8; 1 John 4:8–10; John 15:13); the mysterious necessity for it, evident from Paul's witness in Romans 8:32 that God did not spare his Son but gave him up to death for us, which shows that, he being he, he could not have saved us at any less cost to himself; the mysterious solidarity in virtue of which Christ could be "made sin" by the imputing to him of our answerability and could die for our sins in our place, and we could be "made righteous" before God through faith by the virtue of his obedience (Rom. 5:17–19; 2 Cor. 5:21); and the mysterious mode of union whereby, without any diminution of our individuality as persons, or his, Christ and we are in each other in such a sense that already we have passed with him through death into risen life. Recognition of these mysteries causes no embarrassment, nor need it; since the cross is undeniably central in the New Testament witness to God's work, it was only to be expected that more dimensions of mystery would be found clustered here than anywhere. (Indeed, there are more than we listed; for a full statement, the triunity of the loving God, the incarnation itself, and God's predestining the free acts of his enemies would also have to come in.) To the question, "What does the cross mean in God's plan for man's good?" a biblical answer is ready at hand, but when we ask how these things can be we find ourselves facing mystery at every point.

Rationalistic criticism since Socinus has persistently called into question both the solidarity on which substitution is based and the need for penal satisfaction as a basis for forgiveness. This, however, is naturalistic criticism, which assumes that what man could not do or would not require God will not do or require either. Such criticism is profoundly perverse, for it shrinks God the Creator into the image of man the creature and loses sight of the paradoxical quality of the gospel of which the New Testament is so clearly aware. (When man justifies the wicked, it is a miscarriage of justice, which God hates, but when God justifies the ungodly it is a miracle of grace for us to adore [Prov. 17:15; Rom. 4:5].) The way to stand against naturalistic theology is to keep in view its reductionist method, which makes man the standard for God; to stress that according to Scripture the Creator and his work are of necessity mysterious to us, even as revealed (to make this point is the proper logical task of the word "supernatural" in theology); and to remember that what is above reason is not necessarily against it. As regards the atonement, the appropriate response to the Socinian critique starts by laying down that all our understanding of the cross comes from attending to the biblical witnesses and learning to hear and echo what they say about it; speculative rationalism breeds only misunderstanding, nothing more.

Substitution and Salvation

So far our analysis has, I think, expressed the beliefs of all who would say that penal substitution is the key to understanding the cross. But now comes a point of uncertainty and division. That Christ's penal substitution for us under divine judgment is the sole meritorious ground on which our relationship with God is restored, and is in this sense decisive for our salvation, is a Reformation point against Rome to which all conservative Protestants hold. But in ordinary everyday contexts, substitution is a definite and precise relationship whereby the specific obligations of one or more persons are taken over and discharged by someone else (as on the memorable occasion when I had to cry off a meeting at two days' notice due to an air strike and found afterward that Billy Graham had consented to speak as my substitute). Should we not then think of Christ's substitution for us on the cross as a definite, one-to-one relationship between him and each individual sinner?

This seems scriptural, for Paul says, "[He] loved me and gave himself for me" (Gal. 2:20). But if Christ specifically took and discharged my penal obligation as a sinner, does it not follow that the cross was decisive for my salvation not only as its sole meritorious ground, but also as guaranteeing that I should be brought to faith, and through faith to eternal life? For is not the faith that receives salvation part of God's gift of salvation, according to what is affirmed in Philippians 1:29 and John 6:44, and implied in what Paul says of God calling and John of new birth?[33] And if Christ, by his death on my behalf, secured reconciliation and righteousness as gifts for me to receive (Rom. 5:11, 17), did not this make it certain that the faith that receives

---

33 Rom. 1:6, 7; 8:28, 30; 9:11, 24; 1 Cor. 1:9, 24, 26; Gal. 1:15; Eph. 4:4; 1 Thess. 2:12; 5:24; 2 Thess. 2:14; 2 Tim. 1:9; John 1:12ff.; 3:3–15; 1 John 5:1.

these gifts would also be given me, as a direct consequence of Christ's dying for me?

Once this is granted, however, we are shut up to a choice between universalism and some form of the view that Christ died to save only a part of the human race. But if we reject these options, what have we left? The only coherent alternative is to suppose that though God purposed to save every man through the cross, some thwart his purpose by persistent unbelief; which can only be said if one is ready to maintain that God, after all, does no more than make faith possible, and then in some sense that is decisive for him as well as us, leaves it to us to make faith actual. Moreover, any who take this position must redefine substitution in imprecise terms, if indeed they do not drop the term altogether, for they are committing themselves to deny that Christ's vicarious sacrifice ensures anyone's salvation. Also, they have to give up Toplady's position—"Payment God cannot twice demand / First from my bleeding surety's hand / And then again from mine"[34]—for it is of the essence of their view that some whose sins Christ bore, with saving intent, will ultimately pay the penalty for those same sins in their own persons. So it seems that if we are going to affirm penal substitution for all without exception we must either infer universal salvation or else, to evade this inference, deny the saving efficacy of the substitution for anyone; and if we are going to affirm penal substitution as an effective saving act of God we must either infer universal salvation or else, to evade this inference, restrict the scope of the substitution, making it a substitution for some, not all.

34 Publisher's note: Toplady, "Faith Reviving."

All this is familiar ground to students of the Arminian controversy of the first half of the seventeenth century and of the conservative Reformed tradition since that time; only the presentation is novel, since I have ventured to point up the problem as one of defining Christ's substitution, taking this as the key word for the view we are exploring. In modern usage that indeed is what it is, but only during the past century has it become so; prior to that, all conservative Protestants, at least in the English-speaking world, preferred "satisfaction" as the label and key word for their doctrine of the cross.

The matter in debate might seem purely verbal, but there is more to it than that. The question is whether the thought that substitution entails salvation does or does not belong to the convictional weave of Scripture, to which penal substitution as a theological model must conform. There seems little doubt as to the answer. Though the New Testament writers do not discuss the question in anything like this form, nor is their language about the cross always as guarded as language has to be once debate on the problem has begun, they do, in fact, constantly take for granted that the death of Christ is the act of God that has made certain the salvation of those who are saved. The use made of the categories of ransom, redemption, reconciliation, sacrifice, and victory; the many declarations of God's purpose that Christ through the cross should save those given him, the church, his sheep and friends, God's people; the many statements viewing Christ's heavenly intercession and work in men as the outflow of what he did for them by his death; and the uniform view of faith as a means, not of meriting, but of receiving—all these features point unambiguously in one direction. Twice in Romans Paul makes explicit his conviction that Christ's having died "for" (*huper*) us—that is, us who now believe—guarantees final blessedness. In Romans 5:8–9 he says: "While we were yet sinners, Christ died for us. Much more then, being now justified by his blood, we shall be saved from wrath through him" (KJV). In Romans 8:32 he asks: "He that spared not his own Son, but delivered him up for us all, how shall he not with him also freely give us all things?" (KJV). Moreover, Paul and John explicitly depict God's saving work as a unity in which Christ's death fulfills a purpose of election and leads on to what the Puritans called "application of redemption"—God calling and drawing unbelievers to himself, justifying them from their sins and giving them life as they believe, and finally glorifying them with Christ in his own presence.[35] To be

---

35 Rom. 8:28–39; Eph. 1:3–14; 5:25–27; John 6:37–45; 10:11–16, 27–29; 17:6–26.

sure, Paul and John insist (as all the New Testament does) that God in the gospel promises life and salvation to everyone who believes and calls on Christ (John 3:16; Rom. 10:13); this, indeed, is to them the primary truth, and when the plan of salvation appears in their writings (in John's case, on the lips of our Lord) its logical role is to account for, and give hope of, the phenomenon of sinners responding to God's promise. Thus, through the knowledge that God is resolved to evoke the response he commands, Christians are assured of being kept safe, and evangelists of not laboring in vain. It may be added: is there any good reason for finding difficulty with the notion that the cross both justifies the free offer of Christ to all men and also guarantees the believing, the accepting, and the glorifying of those who respond, when this was precisely what Paul and John affirmed?

At all events, if the use historically made of the penal substitution model is examined, there is no doubt, despite occasional contusions of thought, that part of the intention is to celebrate the decisiveness of the cross as in every sense the procuring cause of salvation.

Substitution and Divine Love

The penal substitution model has been criticized for depicting a kind Son placating a fierce Father in order to make him love man, which he did not do before. The criticism is, however, inept, for penal substitution is a Trinitarian model, for which the motivational unity of Father and Son is axiomatic. The New Testament presents God's gift of his Son to die as the supreme expression of his love to men. "God so loved the world that he gave his only begotten

Son" (John 3:16 KJV). "God is love. . . . Herein is love, not that we loved God, but that he loved us, and sent his Son to be the propitiation for our sins" (1 John 4:8–10 KJV). "God shows his love for us in that while we were still sinners Christ died for us" (Rom. 5:8). Similarly, the New Testament presents the Son's voluntary acceptance of death as the supreme expression of his love to men. "[He] loved me and gave himself for me" (Gal. 2:20). "Greater love hath no man than this, that a man lay down his life for his friends. Ye are my friends" (John 15:13–14 KJV). And the two loves, the love of Father and Son, are one: a point that the penal substitution model, as used, firmly grasps.

Furthermore, if the true measure of love is how low it stoops to help, and how much in its humility it is ready to do and bear, then it may fairly be claimed that the penal substitutionary model embodies a richer witness to divine love than any other model of atonement, for it sees the Son at his Father's will going lower than any other view ventures to suggest. That death on the cross was a criminal's death, physically as painful as (if not more painful than) any mode of judicial execution that the world has seen; and that Jesus endured it in full consciousness of being innocent before God and man, and yet of being despised and rejected, whether in malicious conceit or in sheer fecklessness, by persons he had loved and tried to save—this is ground common to all views, and tells us already that the love of Jesus, which took him to the cross, brought him appallingly low. But the penal substitution model adds to all this a further dimension of truly unimaginable distress, compared with which everything mentioned so far pales into insignificance. This is the dimension indicated by Denney—"that in that dark hour He had to realize to the full the divine reaction against sin in the race."[36] Owen stated this formally, abstractly, and nonpsychologically: Christ, he said, satisfied God's justice

> for all the sins of all those for whom he made satisfaction, by undergoing that same punishment which, by reason of the obligation that was upon them, they were bound to undergo. When I say the same I mean essentially the same in weight and pressure, though not in all accidents of duration and the like.[37]

Jonathan Edwards expressed the thought with tender and noble empathy:

36 Publisher's note: Denney, *Christian Doctrine of Reconciliation*, 273.
37 John Owen, *The Works of John Owen*, ed. William H. Goold (London: Banner of Truth, 1968), 10:269.

God dealt with him as if he had been exceedingly angry with him, and as though he had been the object of his dreadful wrath. This made all the sufferings of Christ the more terrible to him, because they were from the hand of his Father, whom he infinitely loved, and whose infinite love he had had eternal experience of. Besides, it was an effect of God's wrath that he forsook Christ. This caused Christ to cry out . . . "My God, my God, why hast thou forsaken me?" This was infinitely terrible to Christ. Christ's knowledge of the glory of the Father, and his love to the Father, and the sense and experience he had had of the worth of his Father's love to him, made the withholding the pleasant ideas and manifestations of his Father's love as terrible to him, as the sense and knowledge of his hatred is to the damned, that have no knowledge of God's excellency, no love to him, nor any experience of the infinite sweetness of his love.[38]

And the legendary "Rabbi" Duncan concentrated it all into a single unforgettable sentence, in a famous outburst to one of his classes: "D'ye know what Calvary was? what? what? what?" Then, with tears on his face—"It was damnation; and he took it lovingly."[39] It is precisely this love that, in the last analysis, penal substitution is all about, and that explains its power in the lives of those who acknowledge it.

What was potentially the most damaging criticism of penal substitution came not from Socinus but from McLeod Campbell, who argued such by saying that God must punish sin but

---

38 Jonathan Edwards, *The Works of Jonathan Edwards*, ed. E. Hickman (London: Banner of Truth, 1975), 2:575.

39 Publisher's note: See Alexander Moody Stuart, *The Life of John Duncan* (London: Banner of Truth Trust, 1991).

need not act in mercy at all (and in fact does not act in mercy toward all). Reformed exponents of this view reduced God's love to an arbitrary decision that does not reveal his character, but leaves him even in blessing us an enigma to us, "the unknown God."[40] The real target of Campbell's criticism is the Scotist model of divine personality with which, rightly or wrongly, he thought Reformed theologians worked; and a sufficient reply, from the standpoint of this lecture, would be that since the Bible says both that Christ's death was a penal substitution for God's people and also that it reveals God's love to sinful men as such, and since the Bible further declares that Christ is the Father's image, so that everything we learn of the Son's love is knowledge of the Father's love also, Campbell's complaint is unreal.

40 J. Mcleod Campbell, *The Nature of the Atonement*, 4th ed. (London: Macmillan, 1873), 55.

But Campbell's criticism, if carried, would be fatal, for any account of the atonement that fails to highlight its character as a revelation of redeeming love stands self-condemned.

The ingredients in the evangelical model of penal substitution are now, I believe, all before us, along with the task it performs. It embodies and expresses insights about the cross that are basic to personal religion, and that I therefore state in personal terms, as follows:

1. God, in Denney's phrase, "condones nothing," but judges all sin as it deserves, which Scripture affirms, and my conscience confirms, to be right.[41]

2. My sins merit ultimate penal suffering and rejection from God's presence

---

41 Publisher's note: See Leon Morris, *The Apostolic Preaching of the Cross* (Grand Rapids, MI: Eerdmans, 1980), 302.

(conscience also confirms this), and nothing I do can blot them out.

3. The penalty due to me for my sins, whatever it was, was paid for me by Jesus Christ, the Son of God, in his death on the cross.

4. Because this is so, I through faith in him am made "the righteousness of God in him" (2 Cor. 5:21 KJV), meaning, I am justified; pardon, acceptance, and sonship become mine.

5. Christ's death for me is my sole ground of hope before God. "If he fulfilled not justice, I must; if he underwent not wrath, I must to eternity."[42]

6. My faith in Christ is God's own gift to me, given in virtue of Christ's death for me—that is, the cross procured it.

42 Owen, *Works*, 10:284.

7. Christ's death for me guarantees my preservation to glory.

8. Christ's death for me is the measure and pledge of the love of the Father and the Son to me.

9. Christ's death for me calls and constrains me to trust, to worship, to love, and to serve.

Thus we see what, according to this model, the cross achieved and achieves.

CONCLUSION: THE
CROSS IN THE BIBLE

In drawing the threads together, two general questions about the relation of the penal substitutionary model to the biblical data as a whole may be briefly considered.

(1) Are the contents and functioning of this model inconsistent in any way with the faith and religion of the New Testament? Is it degrading to God, or morally offensive, as is sometimes alleged? Our analysis has, I hope, served to show that it is not any of these things. And to have shown that may not be time wasted, for it seems clear that treatments of biblical material on the atonement are often influenced by prejudices of this kind, which produce reluctance to recognize how strong the evidence is for the integral place of substitution in biblical thinking about the cross.

(2) Is our model truly based on the Bible? On this, several quick points may be made as follows.

First, full weight must be given to the fact that, as Luther saw, the central question to which the whole New Testament is in one way or another addressed is the question of our relationship, here and hereafter, with our holy Creator: the question, that is, how weak, perverse, estranged, and guilty sinners may gain and guard knowledge of God's gracious pardon, acceptance, and renewal. It is to this question that Christ is the answer, and that all New Testament interpretation of the cross relates.

Second, full weight must also be given to the fact that all who down the centuries have espoused this model of penal substitution have done so because they thought the Bible taught it, and scholars who for whatever reason take a different view repeatedly acknowledge that there are Bible passages that would most naturally be taken in a penal substitutionary sense. Such passages include Isaiah 53, Galatians 3:13, 2 Corinthians 5:15, and 1 Peter 3:18; and there are many analogous to these.

Third, it must be noticed that the familiar exegetical arguments, if accepted, erode the substitutionary view. The arguments, for instance, for a nonpersonal concept of God's wrath and a nonpropitiatory understanding of the *hilaskomai* word group, or for the interpreting of bloodshed in the Old Testament sacrifices as the release of life to invigorate rather than the ending of it to expiate, only amount to this: that certain passages may not mean quite what they have appeared to mean to Bible students of earlier generations. But at every point it remains distinctly arguable that the time-honored view is the true one, after all.

Fourth, it must be noted that there is no shortage of scholars who maintain the integral place of penal substitution in the New Testament witness to the cross. The outstanding contributions of James Denney and Leon Morris have already been mentioned, and they do not stand alone. For further illustration of this point, I subjoin two quotations from Professor A. M. Hunter. I do so without comment; they speak for themselves.

The first quotation is on the teaching of Jesus in the Synoptic Gospels. Having referred to theories of the atonement "which deal in 'satisfaction' or substitution, or make use of 'the sacrificial principle,'" Hunter proceeds:

> It is with this type of theory that the sayings of Jesus seem best to agree. There can be little doubt that Jesus viewed his death as a representative sacrifice for "the many." Not only is His thought saturated in Isa. liii (which is a doctrine of representative suffering), but His words over the cup—indeed, the whole narrative of the Last Supper—almost demand to be interpreted in terms of a sacrifice in whose virtue His followers can share. The idea of substitution which is prominent in

Isa. liii appears in the ransom saying. And it requires only a little reading between the lines to find in the "cup" saying, the story of the Agony, and the cry of dereliction, evidence that Christ's sufferings were what, for lack of a better word, we can only call "penal."[43]

The second quotation picks up comments on what, by common consent, are Paul's two loci classici on the method of atonement, 2 Corinthians 5:21 and Galatians 3:13. On the first, Hunter writes:

Paul declares that the crucified Christ, on our behalf, took the whole reality of sin upon himself, like the scapegoat: "For our sake he made him to be sin who knew no sin, so that in him we might become the righteousness of God."

---

43 A. M. Hunter, *The Works and Words of Jesus* (London: SCM, 1950), 100.

Paul sees the Cross as an act of God's doing in which the Sinless One, for the sake of sinners, somehow experienced the horror of the divine reaction against sin so that there might be condemnation no more. Galatians 3:13 moves in the same realm of ideas. "Christ redeemed us from the curse of the law, having become a curse for us." [I interpose here my own comment, that Paul's aorist participle is explaining the method of redemption, answering the question, "How did Christ redeem us?" and might equally well therefore be translated "by becoming a curse for us."] The curse is the divine condemnation of sin that leads to death. To this curse we lay exposed; but Christ on his cross identified himself with the doom impending on sinners that, through his act, the curse passes away and we go free. Such passages show the holy love of God taking awful issue in the Cross with the sin of man. Christ, by God's appointing, dies the sinner's death, and so removes sin. Is there a simpler way of saying this than that Christ bore our sins? We are not fond nowadays of calling Christ's suffering "penal" or of styling him our "substitute"; but can we avoid using some such words as these to express Paul's view of the atonement?[44]

Well, can we? And if not, what follows? Can we then justify ourselves in holding a view of the atonement into which penal substitution does not enter? Ought we not to reconsider whether penal substitution is not, after all, the heart of the matter? These are among the questions that our preliminary survey in this lecture has raised. It is to be hoped that they will receive the attention they deserve.

44   A. M. Hunter, *Interpreting Paul's Gospel* (London: SCM, 1954), 31f.

Scripture Index

**CROSSWAY SHORT
CLASSICS**

FOR MORE INFORMATION, VISIT **CROSSWAY.ORG**.